Topics

All the words that appear
in **bold** are explained in the
glossary on page 30.

First published in 1986 by
Wayland (Publishers) Ltd
61 Western Road, Hove
East Sussex BN3 1JD

© Copyright 1986 Wayland (Publishers) Ltd

British Library Cataloguing in Publication Data:
Lambert, David, *1932-*
  Maps and globes – (Topics)
  1. Atlases, British
  I. Title   II. Series
  912   GA130

ISBN 0–85078–624–X

Phototypeset by
Kalligraphics Ltd, Redhill, Surrey
Printed in Italy by
G. Canale & C.S.p.A., Turin
Bound in the UK at
The Bath Press, Avon

Contents

Pictures of the World

The Earth curves out of sight at the horizon.

Suppose you were as small as an ant in a meadow. You would not be able to see over the grass. You would have no idea of the meadow's shape and size. In a way, people are like ants. We cannot see much of the world around us. On land, we cannot see far because trees, hills, or buildings usually block our view. Even on the oceans we can see only a few kilometres – as far as the horizon. For the Earth is almost a sphere, curved liked a ball. Beyond the horizon, the Earth dips down out of our sight.

To glimpse more of the world we should have to climb a mountain or fly high in an aeroplane. Even then we should not be able to tell the exact sizes or positions of places. To learn this you need a **map**.

Maps are special drawings made to help us understand the world around us. A map may use colours, lines, words and **symbols** to show the sizes and positions of things. Many maps show such features as towns, hills, rivers and roads.

Of course, the places shown on maps have to be drawn much smaller than they really are. On a map, two towns 10 kilometres (6 miles) apart may be drawn only 10 centimetres (4 inches) apart.

A reference map showing part of the U.S.A.

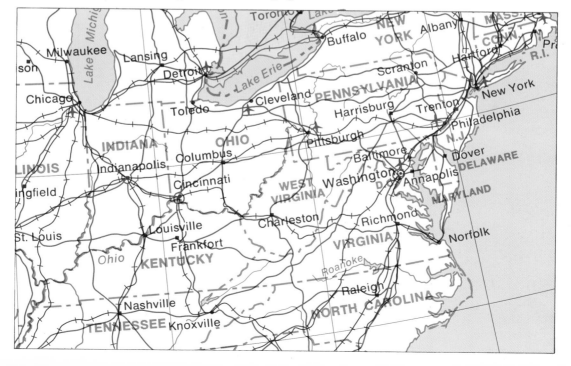

There are two main kinds of map: general reference maps and special maps. General reference maps show such things as towns, rivers, countries and continents. They show where towns and cities are, their sizes, and whether or not they stand on seas or rivers. Road maps are general reference maps for motorists. They show roads and towns but leave out the smaller details which most travellers do not need.

Special maps show particular features. For

A population map of Europe showing the relative sizes of major cities and population density.

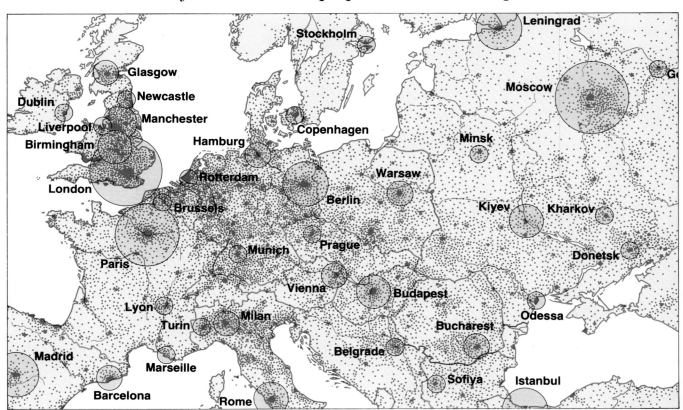

A star chart is like a map of the sky, showing the positions of the stars.

instance, geological maps show the different kinds of rock beneath the ground. Physical maps show the way the surface of the land rises and falls in hills, valleys and plains. Rainfall maps show how much rain falls in various places each year. Weather maps show weather on a given day. Population maps show where the most and fewest number of people live. Political maps show the shapes, sizes and positions of countries.

Not all maps show the land. Maps called hydrographic **charts** show ocean depths and dangerous underwater rocks. Star charts show the positions of the stars in the sky.

This view of the Earth was taken from space.

A collection of maps or charts put together in a book is called an **atlas**.

Maps are flat pictures of the Earth. However, the Earth is not flat but round. If we travelled into space, we would see the whole of our planet. Astronauts, in orbit round the Earth, see the countries and seas laid out on its surface.

To see a picture of what the planet looks like, we need to use a **globe**. Globes are models of the Earth, shaped like a ball, showing the countries and seas looking much as they must do to astronauts out in space.

Understanding a Map

A map will help you to understand the world – if you can read the special language that it uses.

First, to find the real distance between places on a map, you need to know its **scale**. Each centimetre (or inch) on a map stands for a certain distance on the Earth. On a world map, one centimetre might stand for a real distance of 100 million centimetres. The map may give this scale as 1: 100,000,000. Such

A large scale map of Sydney and its suburbs.

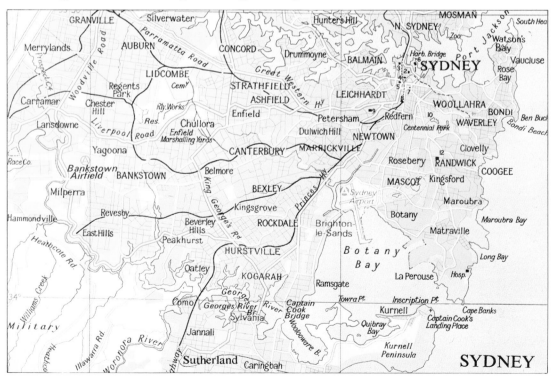

small-scale maps show a large area but not much detail.

For a long car journey you would need a map drawn to a larger scale. The larger the scale, the smaller the area shown. But large-scale maps can fit in many details. A map with a scale of 1: 1,000,000 could include main towns and roads. Maps of 1: 250,000 can also show villages and minor roads. Walkers need maps that give individual fields and footpaths; maps drawn to a scale of 1: 25,000 can picture these.

Maps drawn to the largest scales of all are known as **plans**. Town plans show streets and buildings, and they are used by town planners and workers laying gas or water pipes. House plans show the rooms inside a house. An architect draws a house

An architect's plan of a housing estate.

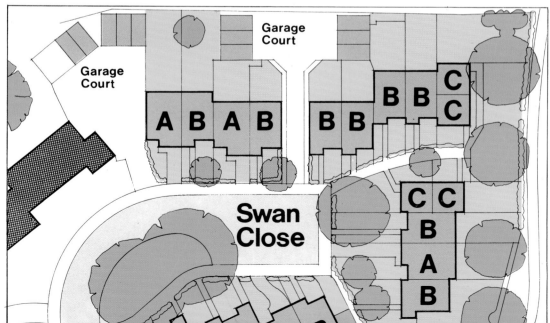

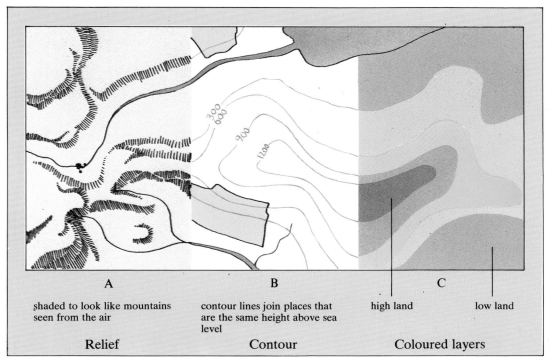

A	B	C	
shaded to look like mountains seen from the air	contour lines join places that are the same height above sea level	high land	low land
Relief	Contour	Coloured layers	

These topographical maps use different methods to show mountains and valleys.

plan as a guide for the builders who will build the house.

    Landmarks such as hills, roads and rivers help you to find your way about the countryside. **Topographical maps** show us these features, using various methods. For example, some of these maps shade hills and valleys so they look quite realistic, like mountains seen from an aeroplane. Other maps show hills only by **contour** lines. These imaginary lines show heights above sea level. A contour line joins up places on the map which are at the same height. The lowest line may show land 10 metres above sea level, the next line 20 metres up, the next 30 metres up, and so on. Many contour lines set close together show a steep hill or mountain. A few lines wide apart show a gradual slope.

Instead of contours, some maps show coloured layers for land at different levels. Usually, low land is green, high land is brown, and the highest mountains are pink or purple.

Topographical maps use many signs or symbols for different landmarks. Blue lines mark rivers.

These symbols can be used on a topographical map.

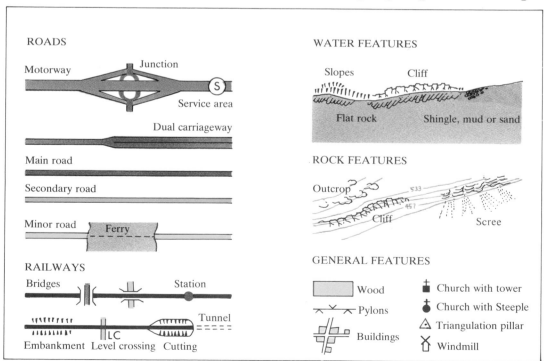

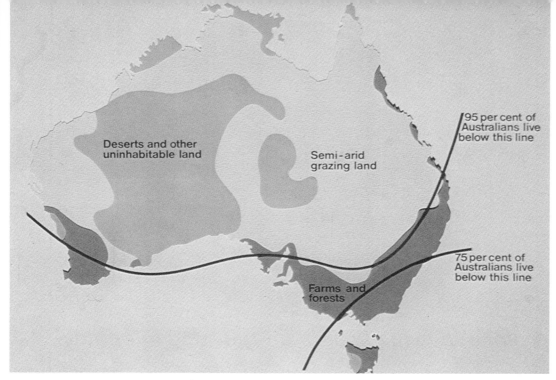

A climatic map showing hot and cold areas.

Variously-coloured lines stand for railways, and different kinds of roads. Other signs or symbols stand for sandy shores, rocky shores, quarries, cliffs, forests, towns, churches, airports, lighthouses, and other items.

Special maps have symbols of their own. On a population map each dot might represent, say, a thousand people. On a flow map, arrows show where goods or people travel. The thicker an arrow, the busier the route. Weather maps have numbered lines called **isobars**. Each isobar joins areas with the same air pressure. Other weather symbols show

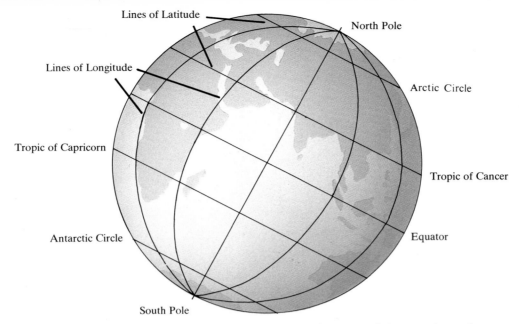

A globe showing lines of latitude and longitude.

such things as clouds, or wind speed and direction. On a climatic map, cold places are coloured white or blue. Hot places are brown or red.

When you plan a trip, your map's scale helps you find the distance you must go. Its signs and symbols help you to find important landmarks on the way. The map also helps to show the direction you must take. On most maps, north is at the top, south at the bottom. West is left and right is east. So if the place you want to reach is above and to the right of where you start from, you know you will be travelling north-east.

On globes and small-scale maps (those showing large areas of land) you can work out the position of places on the Earth's surface using lines of

latitude and **longitude**. The north-south position of a place is shown by lines of latitude. These are drawn across maps and globes from west to east. Each is numbered in degrees north or south of the **equator**.

The east-west position of a place is shown by lines of longitude. These run up and down a map or globe, from north to south. They are measured in degrees east or west of a line drawn through Greenwich, England. Each degree is divided into 60 minutes. Using maps, you can find the position (the latitude and longitude) of any place on Earth.

Large-scale maps (showing small areas of land in great detail) do not show enough of the Earth's

A map of Fiji showing latitude and longitude lines.

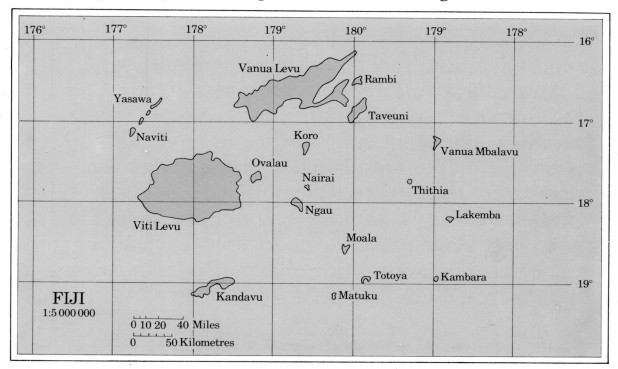

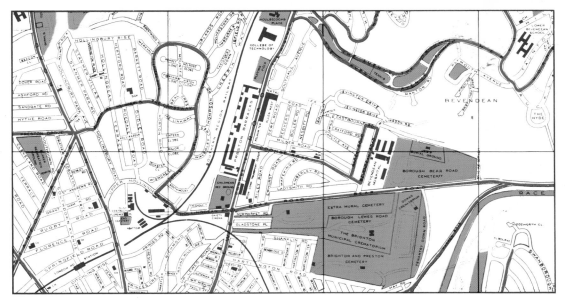

A large-scale street map.

surface for the lines of latitude and longitude to be of much use. So, instead, such a map may be covered by a grid of criss-cross lines, dividing it into squares. The side of each square might, say, represent one kilometre (about half a mile).

Using these squares you can work out the position of any place on the map. A square's position is the number of the line that forms its western edge, followed by the number of the line that forms its southern edge. Often, these squares are subdivided so that you can refer exactly to any point within them. Referring to a place by giving the numbers of its position on a map is called giving it a grid reference.

Globes and Map Projections

Globes are ball-shaped models of the Earth. However, many globes are actually covered by *flat* maps of the world, fitted together in strips. Usually, globes are mounted on a stand so that they can spin round, showing how the Earth rotates as it travels round the sun.

Map projections are ways of showing the Earth's round surface on flat sheets of paper. The name 'projection' comes from a way of using light to

This globe spins showing how the Earth rotates around the sun.

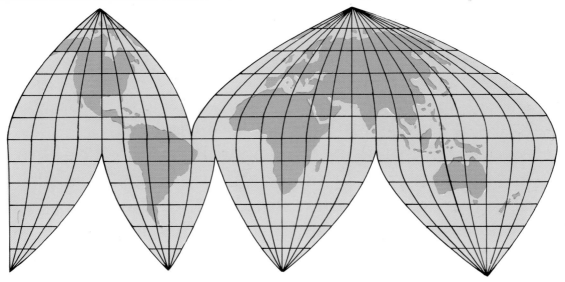

A sinusoidal projection with straight lines of latitude.

project (throw) a picture of a globe on to a sheet of paper. Imagine a lamp inside a transparent globe. If a piece of paper is placed next to the globe, light shining through the globe would project the globe's lines of latitude and longitude on to the paper. These lines could then be copied on to the paper.

Different map projections are made depending on where the light was placed inside the globe and whether or not the paper was lying flat. Instead of being flat, the paper could be curved around the globe to make a cone, a tube, or some other shape. Each arrangement of the light and paper would produce a different kind of map projection.

None, however, would show the Earth's curved surface quite accurately. All projections distort it in some way: areas, directions, distances, or shapes are wrong. Distortion can be very slight on a large-scale map that shows just a town or village. But the error will be much larger on a world map. Yet each projection has some use.

There are three main kinds of map projection: azimuthal, cylindrical, and conic.

Azimuthal projections are made as if drawn on a flat sheet of paper touching a globe at one point in the centre of the map. Some azimuthal projections distort scale, area, and shape so that the countries look almost unrecognizable. But you can use this

The three main map projections.

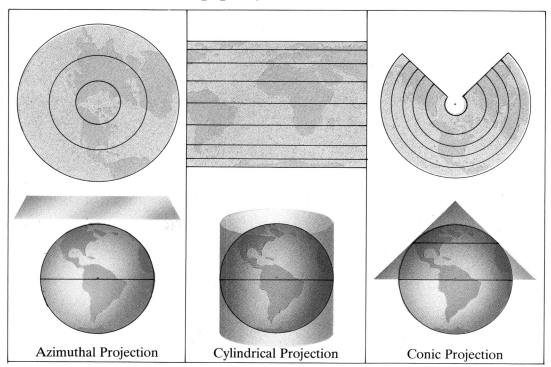

| Azimuthal Projection | Cylindrical Projection | Conic Projection |

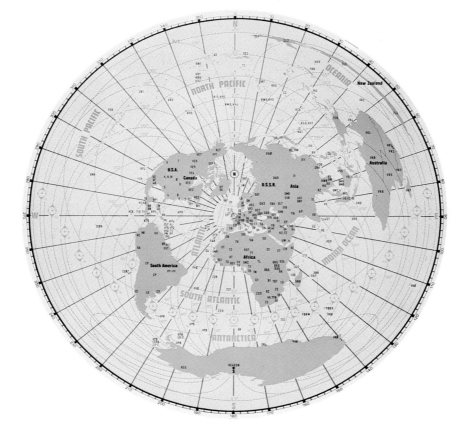

This is a great circle map of the Earth.

projection to show the shortest straight-line distance between two places. This is called a great circle route. Ships and planes can save time by following great circle routes.

Cylindrical projections are made as if you wrapped a piece of paper around the equator of a globe to make a tube or cylinder. The most famous cylindrical projection was invented by Gerardus Mercator in the 1500s. On this projection, lines of longitude do not meet at the **north and south poles**, as they do on a globe. Instead, lines of longitude appear as straight lines at right angles to lines of latitude. This makes northern and southern areas of the globe appear stretched more than areas near the equator. But Mercator's projection shows true wind directions, and ships' captains can use it to draw a compass course between two ports as a straight line.

Conic projections are made as if drawn on a cone of paper wrapped around a globe, touching it along a line of latitude. When the paper is unwrapped and spread flat, it shows lines of longitude meeting at a pole. The lines of latitude appear curved. A conic projection can show areas, distances, and directions fairly accurately. So conic projections are used for many maps in atlases.

The Mercator projection showing lines of longitude at right angles to lines of latitude.

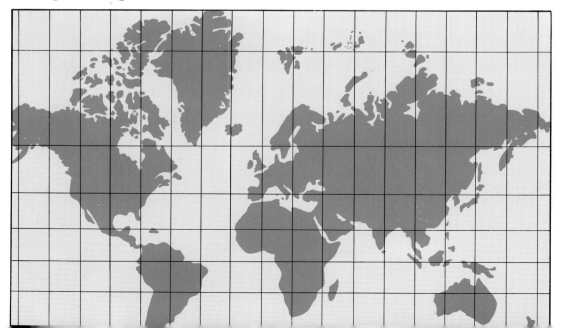

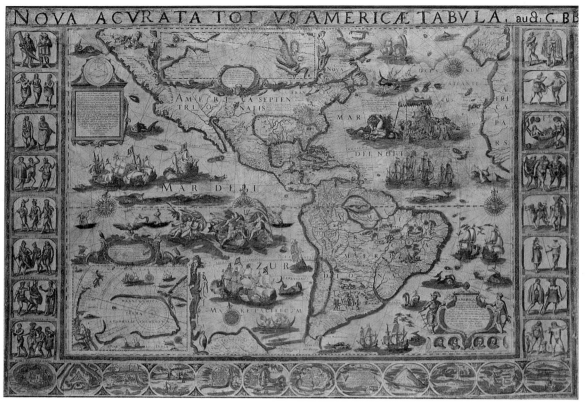

A fifteenth century map of the United States.

Map makers use particular projections depending on what they need to show. Maps showing where the most and fewest people live are drawn to a projection that shows areas correctly. Maps for navigators use projections that show true direction. Projections accurately showing countries near the equator might be wrong for northern lands. A projection that shows a small area well might not work so well for a map that shows a continent.

Making Maps

Before you draw a map you have to find out the exact positions of the places you want to show. This means making a **survey**.

The Greek astronomer Eratosthenes worked out the size of the Earth more than two thousand years ago. But the first accurate survey of a country came

Surveying land in the Sudan which is to be mapped.

Jacques Cassini in the Paris Observatory.

less than three hundred years ago.

In the 1700s, Jacques Cassini surveyed all France. He began by finding the exact north-south and east-west position of two places about 8 kilometres (5 miles) apart. Then he carefully measured the distance between them. This distance formed an imaginary base line. Cassini next measured the angles between the line's ends and a distant church tower. He did this with an instrument called a **theodolite**. This is a telescope fixed to a tripod so it can swing sideways or up and down.

Cassini's theodolite showed the exact position of the church tower. The base line and the lines from its ends to the tower formed a huge imaginary triangle. Each side of this could then become the base line for another triangle using another landmark. In this way Cassini worked all over France, plotting the positions of places. This kind of survey, using triangles, is called **triangulation**.

Using a theodolite in Saudi Arabia.

Theodolites can also be used to find the height of hills. To measure heights above sea level, surveyors use levelling instruments and measuring rods.

Nowadays, surveyors have other tools to help them. For instance, portable radar or radio transmitters help measure distances.

Perhaps the biggest development has been surveying from the air. Aircraft can help to map wild mountain country where surveying on the ground is difficult. To do this, a plane takes two photographs of each piece of ground beneath, from

Portable radars being used by surveyors.

Aerial photographs are used to map wild country.

slightly different angles. When you examine both
photographs through a **stereoscope**, hills and valleys
show up as solid shapes.

Artificial satellites fly far higher than a plane.
Their special cameras help experts to map the
changing weather. Other satellite cameras can see
through fog or mist and send back pictures of

27

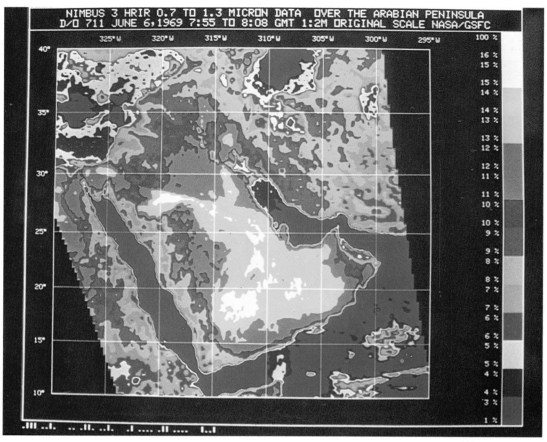

This is a satellite picture of the Arabian peninsula.

forests and deserts for scientists on Earth to study.
Space probes have even carried cameras that
helped to make maps of distant planets. Lasers
have been used to make exact measurements of the
distance between Earth and the Moon.

Meanwhile ships with **echo sounders** have
mapped hills and valleys underneath the sea.

Once, people drew all maps by hand. This was extremely slow. Drawing maps is now much faster, thanks to computers. First, special instruments scan the information in a photograph and turn it into coded numbers that computers understand. Computer-controlled printers or **plotters** can then use these numbers as a guide for drawing coloured lines or patterns. In this way, computers help experts to make maps from photographs.

Drawing a map with the aid of a computer.

Glossary

Atlas A book of maps.

Chart A kind of map, usually showing oceans, stars or weather.

Contour A line on a map, joining places of the same height above sea level.

Echo sounder An instrument for measuring ocean depths.

Equator On maps, a circle drawn around the middle of the Earth.

Globe A model of the Earth.

Isobar Any line on a weather map joining places with the same atmospheric pressure.

Latitude Lines of latitude are imaginary lines around the Earth's surface, parallel to the equator.

Longitude Lines of longitude are imaginary lines running between the north and south poles.

Map A diagram showing where places are on the Earth's surface.

Map projection A way of showing the Earth's curved surface on a flat sheet of paper.

North and south poles Imaginary points at the northern and southern ends of the Earth.

Plan A very large-scale map showing a small area.

Plotter An instrument for drawing maps automatically.

Scale The difference between real distances and how they appear on a map.

Stereoscope An instrument with two eyeglasses. These bring together two flat pictures of a scene so that it looks solid.

Survey Measurement of the exact positions of places.

Symbol A picture or sign that stands for something else.

Theodolite A surveyor's instrument for measuring angles.

Topographical map A map showing natural features, such as hills, and man-made features such as roads.

Triangulation A way of measuring, using triangles to find the exact position of places on the Earth's surface.

Books to Read

Earth Watch by Charles Sheffield (Sidgwick & Jackson, 1981)
Geography edited by Gordon Manley (Macdonald, 1961)
Let's Look at Maps and Mapmaking by Rowland W. Purton
    (Frederick Muller, 1971)
Maps and Map-Making by Mark C.W. Sleep (Wayland, 1983)
The Interpretation of Ordnance Survey Maps and Geographical
    Pictures by B. Lockley (George Philip and Son, 1980)
Understanding Maps by Beulah Tannenbaum and Myra Stillman
    (McGraw-Hill, 1969)

Picture Acknowledgements

Architectural and Planning Partnership 10; John Bartholemew 7, 16; Michael Holford 22; Hunting Surveys Ltd 25, 29; Ordnance Survey 27; Radio Society of Great Britain 20; Ann Ronan Picture Library 24; Science Photo Library 28; J W Wright 23, 26; ZEFA 4, 8, 17. The remaining pictures are from the Wayland Picture Library. The artwork on pages 11, 13, 14 and 19 was supplied by Malcolm Walker.

Index